NORWICH TRAMWAYS

Series editor Robert J Harley

David Mackley

MP Middleton Press

Cover picture: Two generations of tramcar saw service in Norwich. Both are depicted at Silver Road Depot in 1932. In the foreground is car 19, built by Brush for the tramway opening in 1900. On the depot approach line is car 24, built by English Electric in 1925. (Dr. Hugh Nicol/National Tramway Museum)

Published March 2000
First reprinted January 2001

ISBN 1 901706 40 0

© Middleton Press, 2000

Design Deborah Esher

Published by
    Middleton Press
    Easebourne Lane
    Midhurst, West Sussex
    GU29 9AZ
Tel: 01730 813169
Fax: 01730 812601

Printed & bound by Biddles Ltd,
    Guildford and Kings Lynn

CONTENTS

ACKNOWLEDGEMENTS

The quest for photographs for this pictorial record of the Norwich trams has been a fascinating and rewarding experience. It has also provided a context in which to revisit old friendships and to make many new ones.

Peter Larter and Philip Standley kindly gave me access to their extensive collections of pictures and introduced me to other sources. The National Tramway Museum helped with a range of material as well as pictures. Terry Russell provided valuable advice to enable me to prepare tramcar drawings. James Newby, the son of a former tram driver, was able to put names to some of the faces depicted as well as to provide anecdotes. Aileen Fothergill; also from a tramway family, arranged a social gathering of descendents of company staff which produced some fascinating material for this and, maybe, further volumes. I am grateful to the East Anglia Transport Museum for making their historical picture collection available and for encouraging the project. Eastern Counties Newspapers, Jarrold Publishing and the Science & Society Picture Library of the Science Museum kindly permitted use of pictures from their collections, as did the Norfolk Libraries and Information Service (NLIS) to whom I am grateful for access to the George Swain Collection and to Ordnance Survey Maps. The Bodleian Library, Oxford also helped with maps. Pat Lidgett of the Omnibus Society furnished copies of dozens of tickets.

Other valued contributions came from the Lowestoft Maritime Museum, K. Barker, A. Brett, Mrs L. Clapham, M. Dixon, P. Garrod, G. Goreham, B. Gowen, Mrs M. Green, R.Harley, B. Ollington, Mrs J. Parsons, G. Plunkett, C. Temple, S. Tester, M.Vickers, J. Watson, A. Whitwood and A. Williamson. Sadly, Geoffrey Goreham and Clifford Temple died before this book went to print.

I am indebted to my wife, Kathrine, for hours of typing which she assures me she enjoyed!

The last run by a Norwich tram took place nine years before I was born so particular thanks must go to Noel Smith who had encouraged my interest in the Norwich trams nearly 40 years ago.

GEOGRAPHICAL SETTING

Norwich is a major settlement in a predominantly rural area. Ipswich is the nearest town of a comparable size and is in the next county, 42 miles (67kms) to the south. Great Yarmouth lies on the coast, 21 miles to the east. The North Sea is still only 21 miles (37kms) away immediately north at Cromer. Norwich is an amalgamation of smaller settlements which, by late Saxon times, had grown to be one of the five largest towns in England. It lies by a fording point of the River Wensum above its confluence with the River Yare.

East Norfolk is a plateau rarely rising above 300 feet (91.5m) but much of the site of historic central Norwich is perceived from surrounding high points as spread in and around a hollow. Contrary to some under informed references to Norfolk, the City of Norwich is far from flat.

The maps used are 25ins to 1 mile (1:2500) scale reproduced by kind permission of Ordnance Survey. They are from the 1907, 1914 and 1928 editions as indicated.

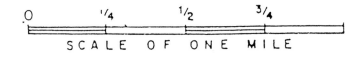

SCALE OF ONE MILE

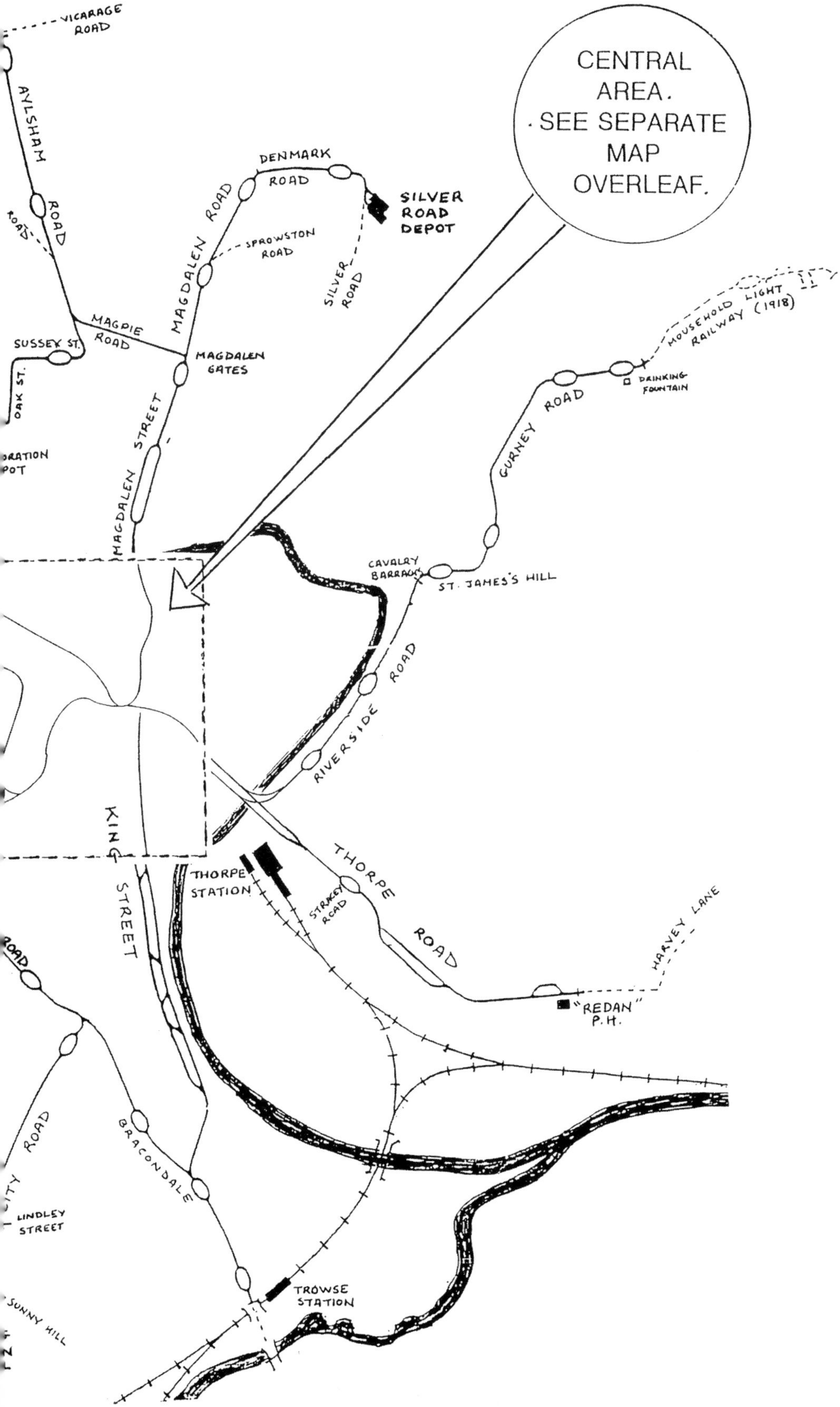

VICARAGE ROAD

AYLSHAM ROAD

ROAD

DENMARK ROAD

MAGDALEN ROAD

SPROWSTON ROAD

SILVER ROAD DEPOT

SILVER ROAD

MAGPIE ROAD

MAGDALEN STREET

SUSSEX ST.

OAK ST.

MAGDALEN GATES

RATION POT

CENTRAL AREA.
·SEE SEPARATE MAP OVERLEAF.

HOUSEHOLD LIGHT RAILWAY (1918)

GURNEY ROAD

DRINKING FOUNTAIN

CAVALRY BARRACKS

ST. JAMES'S HILL

RIVERSIDE ROAD

KING STREET

THORPE STATION

STATION ROAD

THORPE ROAD

HARVEY LANE

"REDAN" P.H.

ITY ROAD

BRACONDALE

LINDLEY STREET

SUNNY HILL

TROWSE STATION

N

HISTORICAL BACKGROUND

When the Normans came, they chose Norwich as their regional capital. By the end of the eleventh century, a fortress had been erected on its mound and a cathedral established. Over the next two hundred years, the city grew and prospered as a chief market town of what was, at the time, one of the most thickly populated areas of England. For a time, Norwich enjoyed the status of England's second city. Significant trades were weaving and leather work. A magnificient collection of churches are a legacy mostly dating from this time. Later trades to come included footwear, brewing, food processing, engineering, banking and insurance. By the mid 19th century, the worshipper still had about 41 parish churches and nearly as many again of other congregations to choose from. Also at this time, the Gospel Temperance Union identified no less than 780 pubs and ale houses!

At the beginning of the nineteenth century, Norwich was still essentially a medieval city with a population concentrated in crowded and often insanitary conditions; mostly within the area described by the old city walls. By 1825, a gradual suburbanisation process began which was well established by 1870. So emerged the need and potential for some means of popular transport between the new residential areas and the economic core of the City.

For a city of such importance, Norwich was a late entrant into the tramway era. The first (horse drawn) service in East Anglia opened between Gorleston and Great Yarmouth in 1875, followed by those at Ipswich and Cambridge in 1880. Various proposals for systems in and around Norwich had been put forward between 1870 and 1887 but not brought to fruition. These had included a scheme set out in 1883 for a cable tramway. Meanwhile, in 1879, the Norwich Omnibus

Company had introduced horse powered public transport but without laying any rails. Eventually, in 1897, a scheme gained Parliamentary approval. So it was that Norwich was to gain the head of the field by opening the new century with the first street tramway in the eastern counties powered by electricity. The successful proponents were the New General Traction Company Ltd, which also owned the Coventry Electric Tramways Company and the Douglas Southern Tramways on the Isle of Man. There were to be considerable similarities between the Norwich and Coventry systems in terms of both infrastructure and rolling stock. Tramcars were to be transferred between the systems on two occasions.

The Norwich Electric Tramways Company was set up in 1897 and was authorised by the City Council to commence construction of the tramways the following year. The city's narrow streets determined the choice of the 3ft 6ins (1067mm) gauge. Major street widening and demolition was required; some of the cost of improvements being shared with the City Council. Most significant were the link through to Castle Meadow, beside the Bell Hotel, and the new access from Redwell Street to St Andrews. Both are still important traffic arteries a century later.

A further major development involved the tearing down of buildings and obliteration of some small streets to make way for Orford Place, a large triangular open space which was to become the hub of the tramway system. The combined effects of wartime bombing and post war redevelopment have since reduced Orford Place to a short length of pedestrian street.

A depot and workshop were provided in Silver Road and a power station installed in Duke Street. The original tramway scheme covered 14.81 route miles (24kms) and

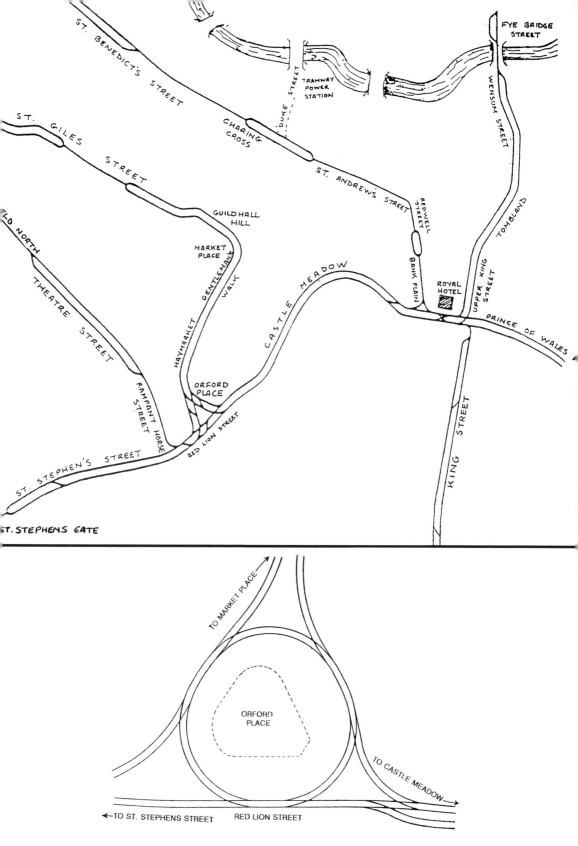

Norwich Central Terminus, original layout.

consisted of 17.5 miles (28kms) of track.

Operations commenced on 30th July 1900 with services to Dereham Road, Earlham Road, Magdalen Road and Thorpe Road. As staff were recruited, further lines were opened to Aylsham Road (1st August), Mousehold via Riverside Road (5th August), Newmarket Road (10th August) and Trowse via King Street on 5th September. The Unthank Road line was at last opened on 13th December. Lines in Magpie Road, Chapel Field Road and Heigham Road were to be used almost entirely as diversions or as short cuts to and from the depot.

Various planned additions to the system were curtailed by the First World War. One unusual development , however, was an extension across Mousehold Heath in the form of an electric light railway to transport materials to aircraft factories. A transhipment spur was laid in at Thorpe railway station. The motive power for this relatively short-lived operation was constructed from tramcar components.The actual track laid across the heath had been salvaged from King Street when the passenger service had closed in 1918.

The trams had linked the Victorian and Edwardian suburbs to the old city within the line of the old City walls. The new council estates and residential areas that grew up after the First World War were beyond the reach of the rails so feeder bus services were inaugurated in the mid 1920s. In 1925, the twisting and tortuous line to Aylsham Road via City Station was closed and a new bus service substituted. Over the same period, a second generation of trams were introduced and some improvements made to track and signalling.

Under the provisions of the 1897 Norwich Tramways Act, Norwich City Council sought, in 1932, to exercise its powers of compulsory purchase of the tramway undertaking which, by then, was running more than 30 motor buses in addition to its 44 trams. Following strenuous opposition from some ratepayers, the matter was put to a poll of citizens. The result was 7,775 in favour of the purchase but 11,033 against. Proponents on both sides of the debate agreed on complete substitution of buses for the trams which, in spite of improvements, were anachronistic compared with the kind of motorbuses by then developed. The point of contention was who was going to pay the conversion bill. The matter stood unresolved until December 1933, when it emerged that the Eastern Counties Omnibus Company had bought a controlling interest in the tramway company. The following year, the necessary legal powers were sought for the abandonment of the trams. Under the subsequent Act, the tramway company became legally The Norwich Omnibus Company, the board of which was composed of City Council and Eastern Counties representatives. This body, which was in no way connnected with the earlier company of the same name, officially ran the Norwich City bus services until 1955, with vehicles technically on hire from Eastern Counties. Tramway abandonment began in earnest in July 1935. The last car, no 10, ran into Silver Road depot on 10th December 1935 amid a noisy throng but without official ceremony. Tickets issued on this last car were printed "Norwich Omnibus Company".

Norwich trams had been regarded with considerable affection and continue to evoke fond memories from those who can recall them. Even so, all the important trends were against the trams by the thirties. Only 29% of those eligible to vote in the 1932 poll had done so. Norwich's civic pride was, therefore, never to extend to a municipally owned public transport system.

ORFORD PLACE

1.   Orford Place is seen shortly after services commenced in 1900. All routes originally started and terminated here. However, a system of cross City routes was soon established. The body of car 39, here depicted, survives. (see 106 & 107). (East Anglia Transport Museum)

←

2.   The track layout was revised in Orford
Place in about 1904. Car 11 from Earlham Road
has been detoured via the avoiding line by way
of Chapel Field North, Theatre Street and
Rampant Horse Street. (K.C. Baker collection)

←

3.   We now look towards Hay Hill and St.
Peter Mancroft Church in about 1910. Orford
Place was a purpose built hub to the tramway
system. The present day Debenham's building
covers most of it.
(George Swain collection/NLIS)

4.   A driver relaxes while two cars on the
same service pause in Orford Place during their
opposite journeys. Just discernible is the pole of
a third car, presumably bound for Thorpe Road.
(Basil Gowen collection)

5.   Who says the English always form an orderly queue? Crowds press for seats at Orford Place in 1913. The occasion was the Norfolk Show being held at what is now Eaton Park. (George Swain collection/NLIS)

6.   A few years later, a car was used as a naval recruitment band-stand in front of Curl Brothers store. Royal Naval Volunteer Reserve officers preside and a Royal Marines Band provides backing. (NLIS)

7.   We remain in Orford Place and look towards the Castle in the early twenties. The cut through to Castle Meadow can be clearly seen. Car 38 awaits departure for Trowse Station (Orange destination board) over the new line via Bracondale. (Noel Smith collection)

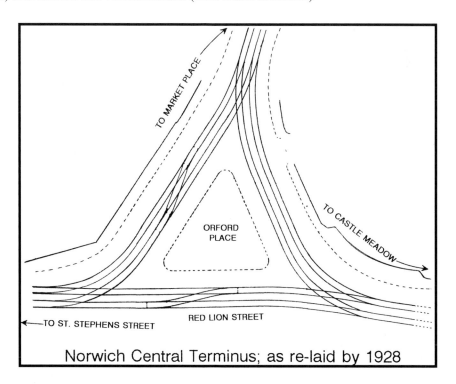

Norwich Central Terminus; as re-laid by 1928

8.   Three cars pause in Orford place in 1932. The building with the clock was a shelter and ticket office erected in 1928. Curls store in the background fell victim to German bombs in 1942. (M.J. O'Connor/National Tramway Museum)

9.   Car 38 squeezes past a lorry parked near the entrance to Lamb Inn Yard. The advertisement for tea is deliciously ambiguous. (H.B. Priestley/National Tramway Museum)

10.   On a quiet morning , car 24 passes the Haymarket and moves on along Gentlemen's Walk. Power was fed to the overhead wires from the column on the left which also supported a rather modest street lamp. One of the older and larger incandescent lamp fittings can just be seen on a column in the middle distance. (Jarrold Publishing)

11.   Gentleman's Walk is shown again, this time looking towards Exchange Street in the 1930s. In this scene of some congestion, 16 motor vehicles, 4 trams, 2 handcarts, a bicycle and numerous pedestrians can be made out! The statue of the Duke of Wellington (left) has since retreated to the relative dignity and tranquility of the Cathedral Close.
(Eastern Counties Newspapers)

12.   A First World War view features car 25 at the stop by the corner of the Market Place. All other non-pedestrian traffic is horsedrawn. Men in khaki mingle with the populace.
(George Swain collection/N.L.I.S.)

13.   The same corner was photographed in the early 1930s. Two English Electric trams pass on Gentlemen's Walk. Motor cars have now appeared; some with rakish lines. The flower stall has borrowed the traction column for display. (Jarrold Publishing)

14.   Another perspective can be enjoyed on the Market Place corner in the 1920s. The Municipal Buildings in the background were demolished when the new City Hall was constructed and the Market Place remodelled in the mid to late 1930s. (Jarrold Publishing)

15.   It is 1917 and passengers use a tram as a viewing gallery, while crowds are exhorted to buy War Bonds by speakers standing on a tank. Tramcars were not permitted to pass on the bend from Guildhall Hill into Gentlemens Walk. (Jarrold Publishing)

NATIONAL WAR BONDS.

Applications received and information given at

LONDON PROVINCIAL AND SOUTH
WESTERN BANK, LIMITED.

NORWICH.

16.   Car 33 descends Guildhall Hill on a summer afternoon in about 1903. The crew can just be seen to be wearing what look like sun helmets. There was a compulsory Board of Trade stop at the top of Guildhall Hill and a 4mph speed limit for the descent. (Lowestoft Maritime Museum)

17.   Car 30 nears the end of St Giles Street in about 1910. All the buildings on the right of the picture were removed in the 1930s to make way for the new City Hall.
(Jarrold Publishing)

top right
18.   A close encounter seems imminent by St Giles Church. Car 25 appears to be conceding the right of way to a Bull Nose Morris emerging from Willow Lane. Although sturdily built, the motor car would have come off worst in any contest. In the far background is St John's Catholic Church, since elevated to the status of Norwich's second Cathedral.
(Jarrold Publishing)

1b 85238

NORWICH ELECTRIC TRAMWAYS Co. Issued subject to Bye laws	**1½d**	St. Bene-dicts Gates	This Ticket to be produced for inspection and given up on demand of an official of the Company.
	Aylsham Road	Cavalry Barracks	
	Brun-dall Road	Ipswich Road	
	Christ Church Rd	Mouse-hold	
	Dereham Road	Orford Place	
	Earlham Road	Thorpe Station	
	Eaton	St. Giles Gates	
	Magdalen Road	St. Clem-ent's ch	
	Thorpe Road	Unthank Road	

19.   St Giles Gate was recorded in about 1910. Car 31 is at the point where the tracks diverge to Earlham Road (left) and Unthank Road (right). Just discernible in the foreground is the line to Chapel Field Road, used mostly as a diversion after 1910. All the nearer buildings have been swept away to make way for a dual carriageway. (Jarrold Publishing)

20.   We take a brief detour to the point where the Chapel Field Road line was joined by another running along Chapel Field North, by way of Theatre Street. This route was used to bypass the Market Place at times of heavy congestion. Trams regained their paths to either Earlham or Unthank Roads at St Giles Gate. Car 29 is posed, not in front of a romantic ruin, but by the Territorial Drill Hall, a Victorian fort-like edifice which incorporated part of the 14th century city wall. A five way traffic roundabout now covers this site. (NLIS)

21.   Retracing our steps to St Giles Gate we find that track and overhead gangs were at work on 8th October 1933. The lines from Chapel Field Road are in the foreground. The then very narrow Grapes Hill is to the right of the hotel. (George Plunkett)

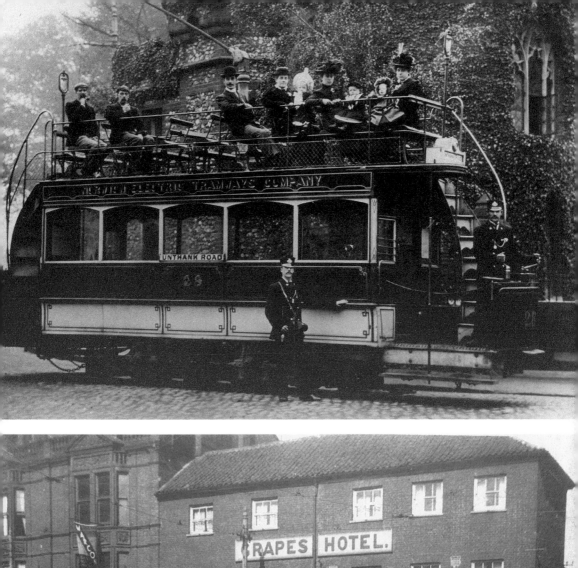

EARLHAM ROAD ROUTE

22.   It is about 1910 and car 10 has encountered a traffic hazard just before the junction for the Heigham Road line. This line was not used for passenger traffic after 1910. The practice of driving livestock through Norwich streets was to outlive the trams and was still common in the 1950s.
(Philip Standley collection)

23.   Car 18, driven by Richard Page, is by the corner of Mill Hill Road in 1935. The column by Carver's Stores had previously supported overhead wiring for the line along Heigham Road. By 1999 it was the sole surviving tramway column in the City and still served as a lamp post.
(Frank Neal/George Swain Collection/NLIS)

24.   Brush car 27 passes the corner of Park Lane in 1929. The destination board's colour is red. A comparison with the next picture illustates the modifications made to nine trams of this type over 29 years. (Dr H.A. Whitcombe/Science Museum, Science and Society Picture Library)

25.   A picture taken soon after the commencement of services shows car 35 drawn up by driver Billy Gamble opposite the corner of College Road. The elaborate window blinds with which these cars were originally fitted can be clearly seen. Sixty years later, Mr Gamble's son made a model of this tram and it is now an exhibit in the Bridewell Museum.
(East Anglia Transport Museum collection)

26.   Earlham Road terminus is seen in this westward view. The original condition of car 6 dates this scene as 1900 or early 1901. The cemetery gates are across the road to the right of the picture. Today, Edwardian terraced houses would be seen from the same vantage point and beyond the gateway behind the tram.
(George Swain collectionNLIS)

27.   Opposite the cemetery gates in the closing days of operation, another car 6 has arrived; this time it is the English Electric replacement of 1927. The conductor is swinging the trolley while the driver switches over controllers for the return journey. Behind the fence were the grounds of a large residence, "Earlham House". Today, this name is perpetuated for a development of shops and flats. (Clifford Temple)

UNTHANK ROAD ROUTE

28.   Overshadowed by the gothic revival grandeur of St John's Cathedral, car 1 turns into Unthank road in the early 1930s. The Austin Nippy has relatively toy-like proportions. The saloon car is entering Earlham Road. (Dr. H. Nicol/National Tramway Museum)

29.   A Brush car has just passed the corner of Clarendon Road in late Edwardian days, leaving the way clear for a tradesman's horse and cart. Tram crews were issued with guidance on dealing with frightened horses in their "Rules for Employees" book. (Philip Standley collection)

30.   CARS STOP HERE WHEN REQUESTED reads the legend on the traction column by the Gloucester St. Post Office (since occupied by a bank). The presence of a steamroller in the distance suggests that the road is about to be metalled. The workmen appear to be clearing the tram rails of mud. (Philip Standley collection)

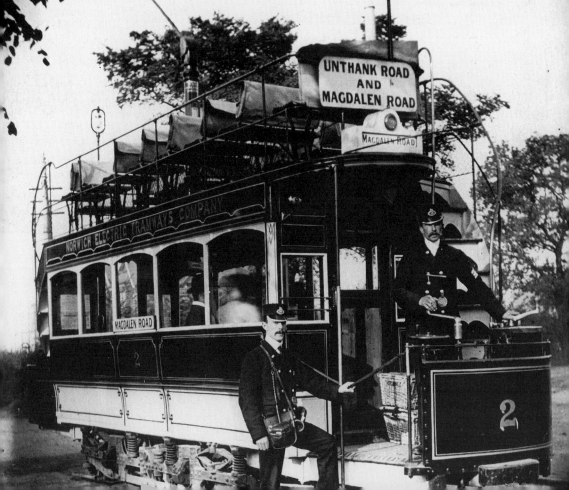

31.   1901 and car 32 has just passed the crossing with Christchurch Road. A horse drawn cart appears to be giving way on the near side but it seems likely that some of its load of hay is about to be dislodged by the tram. (Philip Standley collection)

32.   Car 2 is at Unthank Road terminus in about 1901, shortly after the introduction of coloured route boards (in this case, white), and track brakes (operated by the wheel adjacent to the handbrake). Driver T. Impey and conductor J. Simmonds look purposeful. The rainproof covers for the reversible top deck seats can be clearly seen. Note also the baskets stacked on the platform, possibly being conveyed by the tramway parcels service. The country lane in the background is now the very busy Colman Road. (Eastern Counties Newspapers)

33.   We are at the same spot about 30 years later, but are looking in the opposite direction. There were various permutations of destination equipment applied to the English Electric cars. Car number 1 still has no separate upper deck illumination; night time passengers had to rely on what spilt out from the bulbs in the roller blind route boxes. (R. Neate/National Tramway Museum)

RULES FOR MOTOR-MEN. 35

101.—Motor-men will be expected to become familiar with all the details of the cars, and be able to remedy small faults that may occur on the road. Anyone who does not become familiar with such details will not be retained as a Motor-man. Any man taking interest enough in his work to ask intelligent questions with this view will be appreciated.

102—In passing a vehicle, the horse of which appears frightened, Motor-men must use the *greatest caution*, and bring the car to a standstill if necessary. A horse will frequently be calmed if spoken to gently by the Motor-man.

103—All Motor-men will be expected to assist the Conductor in running each car to time according to the time tables supplied by the Company.

104.—Motor-men in the event of changing their cars at the sheds, must report to the Store-keeper, or in his absence to the watchman, the number of the car they bring in and also the number of the one they take out in its place.

RULES FOR CONDUCTORS. 13

While moving, three bells— "Danger! stop instantly." While standing, three bells— "Back-up."

32.—When a passenger is getting on or off the car the Conductor must not give the signal to start until he or she is safely on or off, and if a lady he must see that her dress is perfectly clear before giving the signal to start.

33.—Conductors must not allow intending passengers to get on their car until those wishing to alight have done so.

34.—Conductors must be ready at all times to give a hand to persons needing their assistance in getting on or off the car.

35.—Conductors must invariably caution passengers against getting off the car while moving.

36.—Conductors must not allow smoking inside their car.

37.—Children must not be allowed to stand on the seats or to damage the cars in any way.

34. It is Edwardian days and a car proceeds from Orford Place via Red Lion Street to the corner of Rampant Horse Street where the elegantly attired ladies are standing. (Philip Standley collection)

→

35. 8.30am on 7th April 1932 and cars are bound for Unthank Road and Earlham Road in Rampant Horse Street, which was part of the avoiding line via Chapel Field. The Market Place was presumably busy with traders' vehicles at the time. (Dr. H. Nicol/National Tramway Museum)

36.　　The junction of St. Stephens Street with Westlegate (left) and Rampant House Street (right) is seen in the early twenties. Turning also to the right is the bypass line seen in the previous picture. Of all the visible buildings, only the grand colonnaded facade of Buntings Store survives today, in the guise of Marks & Spencers. (Jarrold Publishing)

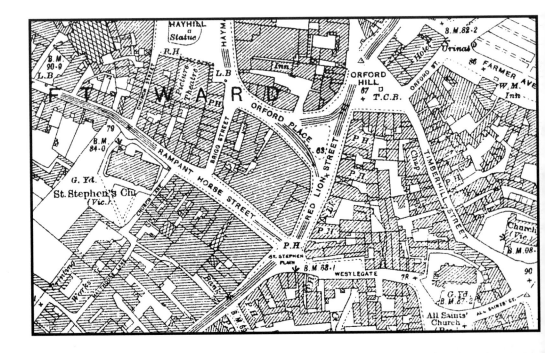

37.   Further up St Stephens Street, in 1899, the new tram tracks (including a crossover) are being laid on a concrete bed. Tie rods and metal sleepers are spaced 2ft 6ins (762mm) apart. (NLIS)

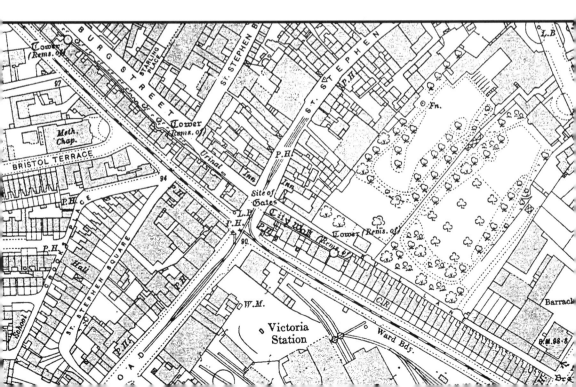

38.　　Car 12 is a little further up St. Stephens Street and about 30 years after the date of the previous picture. It is carrying no destination board and is probably on a positioning journey. The character of this street was changed dramatically by the widening of 1963 in which all the buildings to the right of the picture were swept away. (Eastern Counties Newspapers)

NEWMARKET ROAD VIA ST. STEPHENS ROAD

39.   The Fountain at the junction of Newmarket Road and Ipswich Road was photographed in about 1903. Car 11 proceeds from the City while a returning car waits in the loop by Brunswick Road. Today, a clutter of traffic signals and signs dominates this spot. The large brick canopy has since been demolished. The sculpture of a mother and child that it sheltered was later relocated to the hospital grounds, to the right of the picture. (Noel Smith collection)

40.   Newmarket Road has been described as one of the finest entries into an English city. Car 22 is seen close to the corner of Christchurch Road. The two tone paint scheme applied to the traction standards indicates this to be a very early picture of tramway operation. The octagonal letter box, like the tram, is regrettably no more. (Author's collection)

41.   A scholar from Unthank College (off left background) set up his camera and tripod one December lunch time to take this shot of one of the last "Newmarket" trams passing the corner of Eaton Road. (John Watson)

42.   Newmarket Road terminus was by the junction with Unthank Road. The old school in the background has since given way to a private house. Car 25's destination board is green. The tracks were never extended down the hill into Eaton village, in spite of overtures by some residents. (Philip Standley collection)

TRAMWAY SERVICES.

Eaton to Cavalry Barracks (Colour, Green).—Mondays to Fridays—Cars depart Newmarket Road Terminus at 7.54, 8.4, 8.14, 8.24, 8.34, 8.44, 8.54 a.m., and every 10 minutes until 8.30 p.m., then 8.42, 8.54, 9.6, 9.18 p.m., and every 12 minutes until 10.42 p.m.; then 10.54, 11.6 and 11.14 p.m. to Car Depot only. Saturdays—As Weekdays, but 10 minutes service until 11.14 p.m. Sundays—10.24, 10.44, 11.6, 11.18, 11.30 a.m. and every 12 minutes until 2.18 p.m., then 2.24, 2.34, 2.44, and every 10 minutes until 10.28 p.m., then 10.34, 10.44 and 11 p.m. to Car Depot only.

Cavalry Barracks to Eaton (Colour, Green).—Mondays to Fridays—Cars depart Cavalry Barracks Terminus at 7.49, 7.59, 8.9, 8.19, 8.29, 8.39 a.m., and every 10 minutes until 8.39 p.m., then 8.54, 9.6, 9.18, 9.30 p.m., and every 12 minutes until 10.54 p.m., then 11.8 p.m. to Car Depot only. Saturdays—As Weekdays, but 10 minutes service until 11.8 p.m. Sundays—10.48, 11.8, 11.18, 11.30, 11.42 a.m., and every 12 minutes until 1.54 p.m., then 2.9, 2.19, 2.29 p.m., and every 10 minutes until 10.38 p.m., then 10.55 p.m. to Car Depot only.

Earlham Road to Thorpe Road (Colour, Red).—Mondays to Fridays—Cars depart Earlham Road Terminus at 7.4, 7.12, 7.24, 7.31, 7.39, 7.46, 7.54, 8, 8.6, 8.12, 8.18, 8.24, 8.30, 8.36, 8.42, 8.48, 8.54 a.m., and every 6 minutes until 10.48 p.m., then 10.54, 11, 11.6 and 11.12 p.m. to Car Depot only. Saturdays—As Weekdays, but a 5 minutes service from 9.30 a.m.; Last Cars as Weekdays. Sundays—10.31, 10.46, 10.54, 11.9, 11.16, 11.24, 11.31 a.m., and every 7½ minutes until 1.54, 2, 2.6, 2.12, 2.18 p.m. and every 6 minutes until 8.54, 9.1, 9.9, 9.16 p.m., and every 7½ minutes until 10.31 p.m., then 10.39, 10.45, 10.54 and 10.57 p.m. to Car Depot only.

Thorpe Road to Earlham Road (Colour, Red).—Mondays to Fridays—Cars depart Thorpe Road Terminus at 7.18, 7.29, 7.36, 7.43, 7.50, 7.58, 8.6, 8.12, 8.18, 8.24, 8.30, 8.36, 8.42, 8.48, 8.54, 9.0 a.m., and every 6 minutes until 10.48 p.m., then 10.54, 11, 11.6 and 11.12 p.m. to Car Depot only. Saturdays—As Weekdays, but 5 minutes service from 9.20 a.m.; Last Cars as Weekdays. Sundays—10.28, 10.43, 10.58, 11.13, 11.20, 11.28, 11.35 a.m., and every 7½ minutes until 2.5 p.m., then 2.12, 2.18, 2.24 p.m., and every 6 minutes until 8.30 p.m., then 8.35, 8.43, 8.50 p.m., and every 7½ minutes until 10.33 p.m., then 10.43, 10.50 and 10.58 p.m. to Car Depot only.

Unthank Road to Magdalen Road (Colour, White).—Mondays to Fridays—Cars depart Unthank Road Terminus at 7.4, 7.12, 7.23, 7.28, 7.33 a.m., and every 5 minutes until 10.53 a.m., then 11 a.m., and every 5 minutes until 7.40, then 7.44, 7.49, 7.55, 8.1 p.m., and every 6 minutes until 11.13 p.m. Saturdays—7.4, 7.12, 7.25, 7.30 a.m., and every 5 minutes until 11.15 p.m. Sundays—10.27, 10.37, 10.47, 10.57, 11.7, 11.13, 11.19, 11.25 a.m., and every 6 minutes until 10.58 p.m.

Magdalen Road to Unthank Road (Colour, White).—Mondays to Fridays—Cars depart Magdalen Terminus at 6.36, 6.45, 6.55, 7, 7.10, 7.15 a.m., and every 5 minutes until 7.10 p.m., then 7.16, 7.22, 7.28 and every 6 minutes until 10.46 p.m. Saturdays—6.36, 6.45, 6.55, 7, 7.10, 7.15 a.m. and every 5 minutes until 10.45 p.m. Sundays—10.2, 10.12, 10.22, 10.32, 10.42, 10.46, 10.52, 10.58 a.m., and every 6 minutes until 10.30 p.m.

Dereham Road to Royal Hotel (Colour, Blue).—Mondays to Fridays—Cars depart Dereham Road Terminus at 7.10, 7.24, 7.32, 7.40, 7.48, 7.56 a.m., and every 8 minutes until 10.8 a.m., then 10.15, 10.23, 10.30, 10.38, 10.45, 10.53, 11 a.m., and every 7½ minutes until 11.15 p.m. Saturdays—As Weekdays, but a 6 minutes service from 12 noon to 11.15 p.m. Sundays—10.25, 10.55, 11.25, 11.35, 11.45, 11.55 a.m., 12.5, 12.15, 12.23, 12.30, 12.38, 12.45, 12.53, 1 p.m., and every 7½ minutes until 11 p.m.

Royal Hotel to Dereham Road (Colour, Blue).—Mondays to Fridays—Cars depart Royal Hotel at 6.55, 7.10, 7.18, 7.26, 7.36, 7.44, 7.52, 8 a.m., and every 8 minutes until 10 a.m., then 10.8, 10.15, 10.23, 10.30, 10.38, 10.45, 10.53, 11 a.m., and every 7½ minutes until 11 p.m. Saturdays—As Weekdays, but a 6 minutes service from 12 noon to 11 p.m. Sundays—10.10, 10.40, 11.10, 11.20, 11.30, 11.40, 11.50 a.m., 12 noon, 12.8, 12.15, 12.23, 12.30, 12.38, 12.45, 12.53 p.m., and every 7½ minutes until 10.45 p.m.

Trowse Station to Orford Place (Colour, Orange).—Mondays to Saturdays—Cars depart Trowse Station Terminus at 8 a.m., and every 30 minutes until 11 p.m. Sundays—11.30 a.m., and every 30 minutes until 11 p.m.

Orford Place to Trowse Station (Colour, Orange).—Mondays to Saturdays—Cars depart Orford Place 7.45 a.m., and every 30 minutes until 10.45 p.m. Sundays—11.15 a.m., and every 30 minutes until 10.45 p.m.

City Road to Orford Place (Colour, Yellow and Red).—Mondays to Saturdays—Cars depart City Road Terminus at 8.15 a.m., and every 30 minutes until 11.15 p.m. Sundays—11.45 a.m., and every 30 minutes until 10.45 p.m.

Orford Place to City Road (Colour, Yellow and Red).—Mondays to Saturdays—Cars depart Orford Place 8 a.m., and every 30 minutes until 11 p.m. Sundays—11.30 a.m., and every 30 minutes until 10.30 p.m.

Last Cars from Orford Place.—Weekdays: To all Termini at 11 p.m., excepting Trowse, which leaves at 10.45 p.m. Sundays: To all Termini at 10.45 p.m., excepting City Road, which leaves at 10.30 p.m.

WORKMEN'S TICKETS.—Issued on Cars from 2d., and available only between the following hours, viz.:—Up to 8.30 a.m., between 12.30 and 2.30 p.m., and 5 to 7.15 p.m. Not available on Sundays, Holidays, or after 2 p.m. on Saturdays.

SCHOLARS' TICKETS.—Twelve Tickets, 1/-. Available only between the following hours, viz.:—From 8 to 9 a.m., from 12 noon to 5 p.m. Not available on Sundays, Bank or School Holidays, and after 1 p.m. on Saturdays. Infants in arms free if under 3 years of age.
Children under 12 years of age, Half Fares. No fare less than 1d.

PASSENGERS' PARCELS.—For one article, Minimum Charge, 1d. for 1d. journey, 1½d. beyond.

1929

TROWSE VIA BRACONDALE

43.   Car 12 heads into Queens Road and across St Catherine's Plain in February 1934. The dome-like structure to the right of the picture is a gentlemen's convenience made of cast iron and was referred to colloquially as the 'treacle tin'. (George Plunkett)

44.   The conductor swings the trolley of car 12 at Trowse terminus on 2nd February 1934. This service (orange route board) had only four more days to run. Following the closure of the King Street line in 1918, this new service to Trowse was opened the following year along newly laid track in Bracondale. (George Plunkett)

CITY ROAD ROUTE

45.   City Road was pho-
tographed in about 1910.
The tram in the distance is
on the service to Orford
Place and has a yellow and
red destination board.
(Jarrold Publishing)

46.   Car 21 stands at the
City Road terminus at the
crest of Long John Hill. The
tower of St Marks Church
with its four pinnacles can
just be seen in the distance.
Tramway men Barker,
Bagshaw, Lingley and
Reeve are in attendance
with car 21 about 1902.
(L. Clapham)

ORFORD PLACE TO
ROYAL HOTEL

47.   The gleaming varnished paintwork of Brush car no. 27 suggests that it was newly rehabilitated when this picture was taken at the bottom of Orford Hill in the early 1930s. (George Swain collection/NLIS)

48.   Castle Meadow was a relatively narrow thoroughfare when this picture was taken in the early 1920s. The handcart in the foreground is parked by the entry to Arcade Street. (Frank Neal/ George Swain collection/NLIS)

49.   This scene is from much the same vantage point as in the previous picture but in 1932. The widening of 1926-27 involved the obliteration of public gardens and cutting into the base of the Castle mound which was stabilised by retaining walls. (Dr Hugh Nicol/National Tramway Museum)

50.   Road widening is in progress at the eastern end of Castle Meadow in 1927. An eastbound car follows the old track, while one westbound has use of the new. The demolition to the right was to make way for the imposing new Barclays Bank. (NLIS)

51.   Overhead wires are being installed by the Royal Hotel in about 1899. The tower wagon was subsequently retained for maintenance purposes. (NLIS)

52.   Cars navigate around an elegant gas lamp by the Royal Hotel. The car on the left will take the sinuous route to Aylsham Road via City Station. 18 and 19 could be heading for Thorpe Road, Magdalen Road or, possibly, Trowse by way of King Street via a right turn beyond the classic portico of the Post Office, which is now occupied by Anglia Television.
(National Tramway Museum)

53.   The busy junction by the Royal Hotel is seen in about 1905. A points boy was permanently stationed at this busy intersection but, in this view, an inspector holds a point iron in the middle foreground. Car 39 is on a short working from Orford Place to Magdalen Road while 31 is making for Aylsham Road from Thorpe Station. (Author's collection)

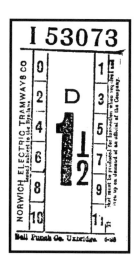

54.   English Electric car 47 is about to clear the points for the left turn into Upper King Street while an older Brush car is about to emerge from the same street and is running in the opposite direction. The lorry load of corrugated drums looks like a mishap on its way to its own occurrence. (Jarrold Publishing)

ROYAL HOTEL TO
DEREHAM ROAD

55.   An Edwardian view of the intersection of Westwick Street with St Benedicts Street and Charing Cross. The buildings to the right have since gone. Otherwise this scene remains substantially unchanged. When car 27 reaches Barn Road, it will take the first of four tight turns en route to Aylsham Road.
(Basil Gowen collection)

56.   Car 18 is in an encounter with an Austin Seven outside Bretts china and hardware shop at 35 St Benedicts Street. In spite of the inconvenience and delay, good nature seems to prevail. (Arthur Brett)

57.   Driver Adams is at the controls as car 18 passes St Benedicts Gate at the junction with Barn Road and Grapes Hill. Mr Fred Baldwin's Austin dairy van looks set to overtake on the inside! Until 1925 there was a junction here for the service to Aylsham Road via City Station. This location was laid waste by German bombs in April 1942 and further transformed by the construction of the Inner Ring Road. (Frank Neal/George Swain collection/NLIS)

58.   Car 33 is at the eastern extremity of Dereham Road and on the approach to St. Benedicts Gate. The buildings in the background also fell victim to the 1942 Blitz. (Clifford Temple)

59.   Car 45 is running out of the passing loop and into the single track section by Nelson Street in the late 1920s. Another English Electric car waits in the next loop. It would not be advisable to propel a wheelchair in this carriageway today. (Jarrold Publishing)

60.   A First World War picture includes Clippie Gladys Beaumont and Brush car 33 at the Dereham
Road terminus. (Courtesy L. Clapham)

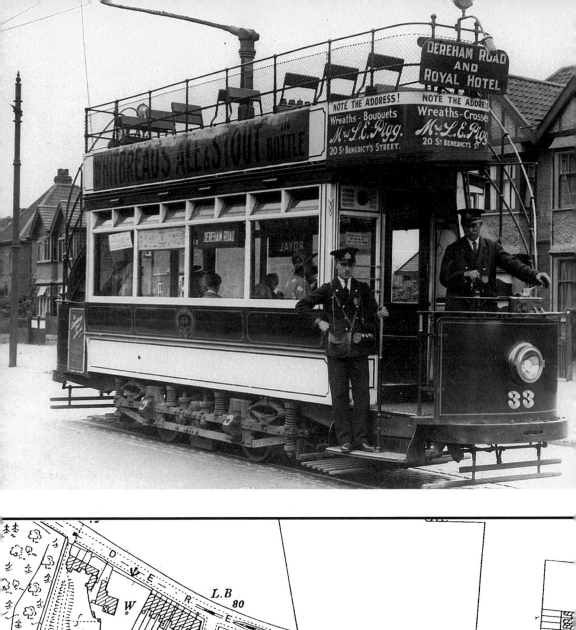

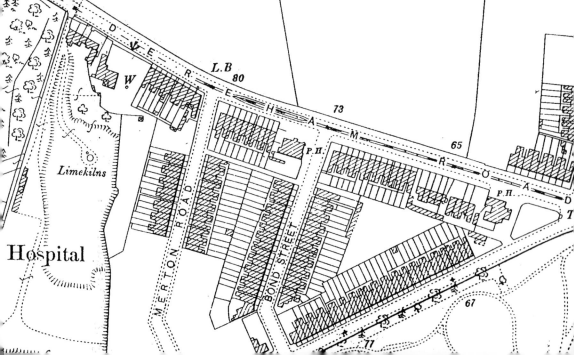

61. Housing looks well established in this lovely study of successor English Electric car 33 at the same spot as the previous picture, probably in 1935. The body of this car ended its days as a farm shed at Winfarthing, Norfolk. (Frank Neal/George Swain collectionNLIS)

62. Car 22, with driver Billy Mack in charge, is at Dereham Road terminus in 1900. Terraced housing on the south side of the road begins an urban encroachment into an otherwise still very rural setting. (Geoffrey Goreham collection)

63.   The same location in 1929 and English Electric car 43 stands at the terminus, by Merton Road. The roadway has been widened and detached villas have grown up in the former field since the previous photograph was taken. Does the smiling cyclist think that he is the subject of the photograph? (Dr H.A. Whitcombe/Science Museum/Science & Society Picture Library)

TROWSE VIA KING STREET

64.   The service via King Street was an early closure and the tracks were removed in 1918. Pictures of trams in King Street could not be found but this wintry scene includes the overhead near the Music House, now part of the Wensum Lodge Educational Centre.
(Mrs A. Davey collection/Mrs J. Parsons)

65.   Car 8 at is Trowse terminus (Bracondale) about 1901. The driver sporting a button hole is George Hill who was to drive the very last Norwich tram in 1935. The body of number 8 ended up in a garden quite close to the car sheds. It gradually disappeared as kindling in the bitter winter of 1963! (East Anglia Transport Museum)

MAGDALEN ROAD ROUTE

66.   At the close of the old century and in anticipation of the dawn of the next, track is being laid by the Royal Hotel at the intersection of Upper King Street, Agricultural Hall Plain and Prince of Wales Road. The strange contraption on wheels is the cupola cart in which molten cast iron was prepared for the Falk welded rail joints. (NLIS)

67. Upper King Street by the corner of Bank Street and an unidentified tram has drawn an interested crowd. The occasion is almost certainly a test run or Board of Trade inspection before the inauguration of regular services. (Percy Garrod coll.)

68. The Erpingham Gate can be seen in the right distance of this view of ancient Tombland in about 1901. The glazed cabin to the right is one of a number of cabmen's shelters that were to be found in various locations about the city before World War I. (Philip Standley collection)

69.   Seen from the Cathedral precincts, the passage of a tram is framed by the Erpingham Gate in about 1905. All buildings in this scene survive today , including the rather geometrically eccentric Augustine Steward House in the far background. (Jarrold Publishing)

70.   Car 46 is seen entering Fye Bridge street from Tombland in the early 1920s, in deep shadow. 46 is one of the motorised matchbox (trailer) cars. The points just behind the tram became very worn in later years causing driver Bertie Newby's car to leave the tracks completely and head for the Erpingham Gate, (to the right). Score marks remained until the wood block surface, seen in the foreground, was replaced. (Jarrold Publishing)

71.   Fye Bridge was widened in 1933, one half being dealt with at a time. Top deck passengers on car 3 stand up to get a better view of the reconstruction works. The children have already seen plenty of this and find a new interest in George Plunkett's Ensign Carbine camera. (George Plunkett)

72.   Cars were stranded in Magdalen Street on Boxing Day 1906. Fourteen inches of snow fell between midnight and 7.00am bringing the tramway system to a standstill. Magdalen Street was part of the main dispersal route from the car depot. Residents were roused by a prolonged rumble each morning and were 'lullabyed' by a similar performance late at night. (East Anglia Transport Museum)

73.   This very early view of car 32 is at Stump Cross, Magdalen Street. The route box indicates LITTLE ORFORD STREET, soon to be referred to as "Orford Place". (NLIS)

74.   Magdalen Road is seen near Shipstone Road in about 1904. A new passing loop is being laid, a very labour intensive exercise involving total possession of the highway and a semi-captive audience. (Ken C Baker collection)

75.   From halfway along Denmark Road, thirteen trams are parked in the open; probably while the depot was the subject of building works. (Tony Williamson collection)

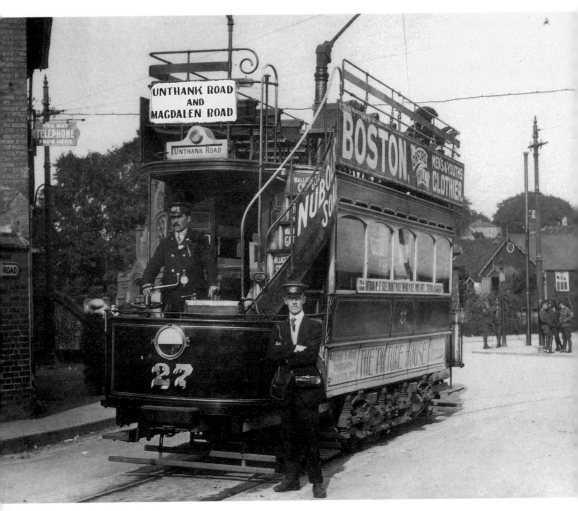

76.   The Magdalen Road route actually terminated at the eastern end of Denmark Road and a few yards from the depot in Silver Road. Ginger Moore is conductor in this First World War picture. The car headlight has been partially masked for the blackout and the military are in evidence on the corner of Gertrude Road. (Philip Standley collection)

77.   The same location in 1935 and car 40 catches the afternoon sun. Contracts for advertising on trams were by then running out, which is why car 40 carries plain livery. (Dr. H. A. Whitcombe/Science Museum/Science & Society Picture Library)

78.   Car 10 is at the junction of Aylsham Road and Drayton Road in about 1910. The fine house in the fork of the roads, and the timber yard behind, have since given way to landscaping and lock up garages. (Peter Larter collection)

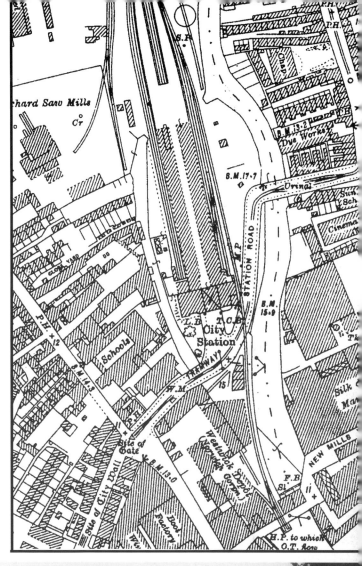

The 1928 survey shows that the line to Aylsham Road via Oak Street crossed a siding from City Station. This siding served the City Engineers Depot and a coal drop for loading river craft at New Mills.

79. Aylsham Road terminus is seen looking north in about 1909. Car 43 is one of the five trailers converted to powered cars in 1906. Its shorter length was an advantage when negotiating the sharp bends encountered on this route which was converted to bus operation in 1925.
(East Anglia Transport Museum)

80.   Aylsham Road terminus and Vicarage Road are pictured in about 1901. Car 25's destination board is blue and red. The side destination board reads CITY STN & AYLSHAM RD. CITY & THORPE STN. Pillbox hats, seen here, were being replaced by flat caps by about 1904. The driver's coat has arm stripes, awarded for seniority of service.
(East Anglia Transport Museum)

PRINCE OF WALES ROAD

81.   Prince of Wales Road in the early 1930s and Car 10 is heading for Thorpe Road, while car 4 climbs past the Royal Hotel en route to Newmarket Road. (Jarrold Publishing)

82.   In the Prince of Wales Road in about 1905, all the vehicles have iron or steel rimmed wheels, but the child in the push chair has the benefit of rubber. (Jarrold Publishing)

83.   Car 37 passes a railway parcels delivery van on the approach to Foundry Bridge in this very early picture. Prince of Wales Road and the bridge were constructed in Victorian times as a grand approach to Thorpe Railway Station. (Philip Standley collection)

84.   Car 25 pauses on Foundry Bridge in about 1901. The Riverside Road and Thorpe Road lines met to the right of the picture. The combination of traction column and gas lamps was an unusual feature for Norwich. (Brian Ollington collection)

THORPE ROAD

85.   The city end of Thorpe Road and the impressive Thorpe Station facade were photographed in about 1902. All the males facing into the picture, including the conductor of car 4, are more interested in the camera than in assisting the young ladies with the trunk. (Philip Standley collection)

86.   The outward end of the Mousehold Light Railway transhipment spur in Thorpe Station forecourt is seen in April 1935. It remained in situ until the 1950s. No service trams ever entered the station precincts although passenger cars are known to have been used for crew transport on the light railway.

(Dr Hugh Nicol /National Tramway Museum)

Gf 01848

NORWICH ELECTRIC TRAMWAYS Co. Issued subject to the Bye-laws.	**1d.**	Oxford Place	This ticket must be produced to the Inspector when required and gives up on demand	
	Aylsham Road	Eaton		
	Branksome Rd	St Clement's Ch		
	City Road	Thorpe Station		
	Christ Church Rd	Crown Brewery		
	Earlham Road	Cavalry Barracks		
	Unthank Road	St Giles Gates		
	Dereham Road	St Benedicts Gates		
	Magdalen Road	Ipswich Road		
	Thorpe Road	per St. Gates		
	Trowse	Royal Hotel		
	Mouseh'ld Heath	**1d.**		

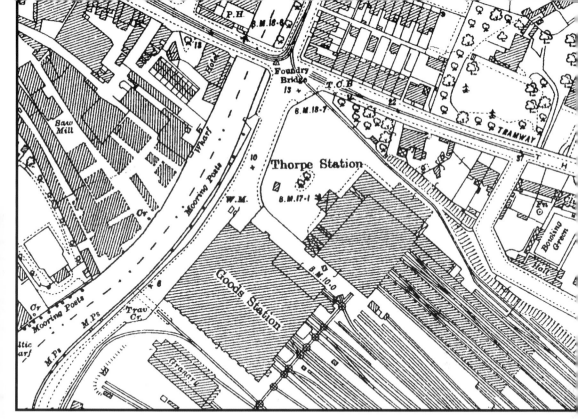

87.　　Outside the station forecourt, we witness a gloomy winter view full of incident and detail. Passengers and cyclists tangle by the car bound for the City and Earlham Road. Just above the car are the feeder cables for the overhead traction wires. An Eastern Counties bus with a "tin bible" route indicator is entering the station yard and dates this picture as 1931 or later. Car 9 is one of the two more powerful Mousehold cars. (R.B. Parr/National Tramway Museum)

88.   Rosary Corner in about 1920 and car 13 approaches the spread in the overhead wires for the passing loop. All this hardware and the iron railings have since gone. Otherwise, this setting is recognisable today.
(Basil Gowen collection)

89.   The corner of Matlock Road around 1905 and car 36 carries a green destination board for the service to Newmarket Road. Thorpe Road trams later ran to Earlham Road (red route board). The Thorpe Road terminus, by The Redan public house, was about 300 yards behind the tram.
(Tony Whitwood collection)

90.   Thorpe Road terminus was by The Redan public
house and is seen on 16th April 1935. The last tram to
set off from here ran three months later.
(Dr. Hugh Nicol/National Tramway Museum)

RIVERSIDE ROAD AND MOUSEHOLD

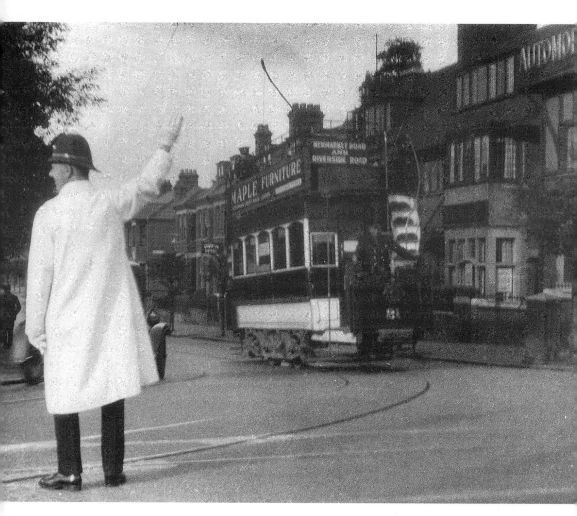

91.   Car 21 with its green destination board waits in Riverside Road for
the right of way to turn over Foundry Bridge and into Prince of Wales Road
in about 1930. The points for the junction with the Thorpe Road line can
be seen by the policeman's feet.
(M.J. O'Connor/National Tramway Museum)

92.   In the Summer, the Riverside Road service was extended beyond the Cavalry Barracks to Mousehold Heath. Here, Gurney Road is seen in Edwardian days. On the right, Britannia Barracks looks down on car 13 descending, while, in the distance, another car approaches the last major bend before the Summer terminus. (Philip Standley collection)

93.   The view from almost the same vantage point is from 6th May 1935. Three cars handle crowds enjoying a special day's holiday to commemorate King George V's Silver Jubilee. In a quarter century, many saplings have become mature trees. (George Plunkett)

94.   The Fountain at Mousehold Heath is where car 14 is depicted in this picture postcard view from about 1901.   From this spot, the 1918 Mousehold Light Railway continued, from the left of the picture, at first along the road and then through a shallow cutting on the heath, to aircraft and munitions factories at Roundtree Corner. (Philip Standley collection)

SILVER ROAD DEPOT

95.   The Silver Road Depot and workshops comprised two four-road sheds. The south shed is seen in 1949. Originally all the doorways were arched. Most were modified to give clearance for the longer upper decks of the new English Electric cars in the 1920s.
(A.P. Cooper/National Tramway Museum)

96.   Five cars were in the south shed on 5th April 1932 - left to right 42, 24, 30, 21, 45. Car 24 stands partly in the workshop area. Car 21 is also on a workshop road.
 (Dr. Hugh Nicol/National Tramway Museum)

97.   We look inside the workshop in April 1932. In the background are a forge and an array of tools. In the foreground is the wheel lathe with a wheel tyre leaning against it.
(Dr. Hugh Nicol/National Tramway Museum)

Elevation of rail showing position of ties and tie rods.
(Tramway & Railway World)

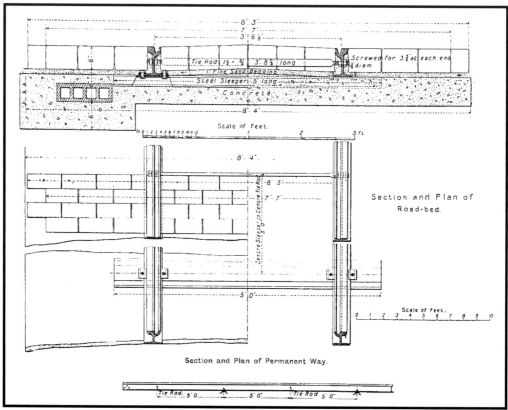

TRACK AND OVERHEAD

Installing a tramway in a medieval street pattern presented some challenges, including recourse to some very sharp curves and appreciable gradients in places. Comparatively light 65.5lb Belgian rail was used on the straights and 90 lb on the curves. This was clipped to steel sleepers alternating with tie rods at intervals of 2ft 6ins (762mm). An interesting feature was the use of rail joints welded by the Falk process. This was expensive but it enabled the use of much lighter (and consequently cheaper) rail than would be required for bolted joints.

The overhead wire was supported by a range of methods depending on the location. Side poles with span wires suspended across the road were common. Side poles with bracket arms were used mostly on single line sections. Centre poles with brackets each side were set down the middle of Prince of Wales Road. Wall rosettes, from which span wires were suspended, were attached to sturdier buildings in narrow streets, where space for poles was limited. In 1998 more than 25 were still in situ, including one attached to the historic Guild Hall.

98.   Track is being laid on Tombland adjacent to the Maids Head Hotel. The alternating metal sleepers and tie rods can be clearly seen. (Howard collection/NLIS)

99.   A Falk welding mould and clamps are seen applied to a joint in the original track installation in Dereham Road. The use of the lighter gauge rail with welded joints was not perpetuated when additions or alterations to the track layout were required.
(East Anglia Transport Museum)

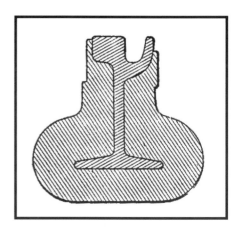

A contemporary account of rail welding stated:
All rail ends on the new tracks have been cast welded on the Falk system by Messrs. R. W. Blackwell and Company. The rail ends are first cleaned and placed firmly together, or, if this is impossible, thin plates of steel are driven in between the heads of the rails before casting. A cast iron mould is then placed around the sides of the head, the web, and the base of the rail, which has been thoroughly cleaned by an emery wheel or sand blast. The mould has an opening at the top for pouring in the metal. A cupola cart, in which the metal for casting is heated, is brought up, and the metal, which is of special chemical composition to give good results, is run in at a greater heat than is usual in making castings. The cast iron running into the mould cools rapidly on the outside surface, thus causing great pressure to be exerted on the metal that is still in its molten state in contact with the web and base of the rail, which are brought to a white heat, and owing to the pressure on the molten cast iron this is forced into the interstices of the steel. Actual fusion on the rail and cast iron cannot take place, but the result, after cooling, is a very tight joint. Any unevenness on the upper surface is then ground away to leave a smooth surface. (Tramway & Railway World)

The process was expensive and not widely adopted elsewhere. However, it was reckoned that, with the use of a light section rail with a heavier head than was customary, as much wear could be got out of a 65.5lb rail as out of a much heavier rail with ordinary joints.

100. A portable track grinder was invented by Mr Alan Banister, the first General Manager. Power was taken from the overhead via a flexible cable attached to a bamboo pole.
(Tramway & Railway World)

Three main types of traction column:
(1) Side pole for span wires
(2) Centre pole for double tracks
(3) Side pole with bracket arm

Double wires were installed over the busier single line sections to obviate the need for frogs at passing loops.

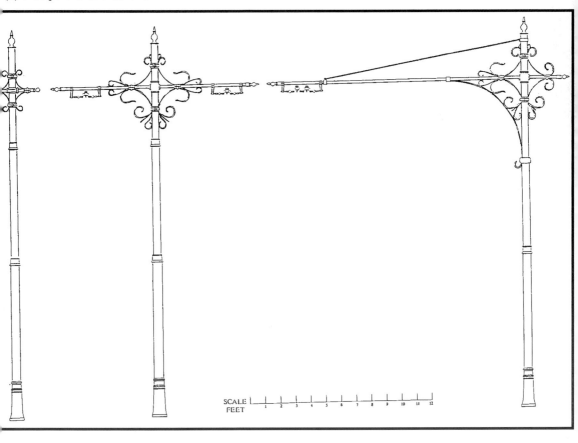

SCALE
FEET

1 2 3 4 5 6 7 8 9 10 11 12

ROLLING STOCK

The original tram fleet of 1900 consisted of fifty open top cars of which ten were unpowered trailers. All were of a similar appearance with bodies by Brush of Loughborough. The powered cars, numbered 1-·40, had Westinghouse electrical equipment and Peckham cantilever trucks. They seated 52 passengers. The trailers, numbered 41-·50, were shorter, having four arched side windows instead of the larger cars' five. They seated 40 passengers. Both types were virtually identical to smaller batches supplied a year earlier to the associated Coventry Electrical Tramways Co. Two of the Coventry powered cars were transferred to Norwich in 1904 where they took the numbers 41 and 42 from two of the trailers which were then renumbered 51 and 52.

The 42 Brush powered cars underwent a series of modifications over a period of twenty or more years. These included the fitting of track brakes, new life guards, upper deck side panels and electric head and tail lamps. The short wheelbase and long end overhang precluded the addition of the weight of canopies, vestibule screens and top covers.

In 1906 five cars were fitted with Mountain & Gibson radial trucks which, in theory at least, enabled a longer wheelbase to negotiate sharp curves. The experiment was not a lasting success and similar equipment used elsewhere is known to have become troublesome. In 1910, all five cars were transferred to (or literally sent to) Coventry where, after modification, they were to give a further 30 years service.

There is little record of the use of the trailers in Norwich. Evidently, they were not a success, either operationally or economically. When the radial truck experiment of 1906 released five sets of traction equipment from larger cars, numbers 43-47 were converted to powered operation. They were largely allocated to secondary duties and the winding route to Aylsham Road via Oak Street, Sussex Street and St Augustines Street. Of the remaining five trailers, one was converted to a track gang van and the others cannibalised.

In 1918, the Company constructed on behalf of the Government some powered goods tractor units and trailers for the Mousehold Light Railway. All were mounted on secondhand tramcar trucks, mostly of the Peckham cantilever type. The tractor units were fitted with BTH controllers and 38hp motors. The Light Railway closed with the cessation of hostilites and the rolling stock was advertised. This enabled the company to obtain sufficient traction equipment for installation in two new trams. These appeared in 1923 and took numbers 7 and 9 left by two of the cars exiled to Coventry. The 55-seat bodies were built by English Electric at Preston. These cars were allegedly referred to by crews as "Dreadnaughts", presumably because they were the most powerful cars in the fleet. They were also called "Mousehold cars", possibly on account of their history but also because their greater power suited them for the climb over the Heath.

From 1924 onwards, further outwardly identical English Electric cars were supplied to replace the Brush cars. They had new Dick Kerr type controllers but were fitted with rehabilitated trucks and motors from their predecessors. Each truck retained its number and took it to its new car. Four of the five trailer/motor conversions were the first candidates for this reincarnation process. Over the next six years all but nine of the standard Brush cars were replaced, including the two ex-Coventry examples. After some rebuilding, the remaining Brush cars continued in service until the closing months of operation.

The company livery was dark maroon and ivory (a broken white). Originally, the maroon waist panels and dashes were lined out with a half inch gold line and a narrower line of white. The ivory was lined in combinations of maroon and black. The lining was arranged in decorative panels on the car sides and in elaborate motifs on the corner pillars. The company name was carried above the side windows in large gold shaded letters. A bold fleet number was applied to each dash panel and smaller ones to the car sides. Trucks and other running gear were painted red.

A simplified livery was introduced with the arrival of the English Electric cars. The gold and white lines gave way to a single half inch yellow line. Fleet digits were smaller and the company name appeared in an oval belt and buckle device on the car sides. Trucks and running gear were now painted black or grey.

The maroon is known to have darkened in use, probably the combined result of ageing and the use of successive coats of varnish. Some observers, therefore, recalled a chocolate hue. Norwich trams do not seem to have succumbed to a down at heel look and were well turned out until the last.

101.   Brush car number 5 is on the depot forecourt, as delivered in 1900. This is the only photograph traced by the author showing a Norwich car fitted with drawbars for trailer operation. These fittings seem to have been removed at a very early stage. (National Tramway Museum)

102.   No. 41 was one of two cars transferred from Coventry Electric Tramways in 1904; it had been Coventry car 19. The Coventry livery was almost identical to that at Norwich and close examination of this photograph reveals that car 41 has been given a "touch over", rather than a full repaint. By about 1904, all Norwich trams had new "gate and tray" lifeguards under the platforms. The fitting of top deck side panels began the same year. (George Swain collection/ NLIS)

103. By about 1906, upper deck decency panels had been fitted to all cars and longer destination boards were in use. Widened outer stair stringers provided advertising space as did each individual stair riser! The lower side panels also often carried advertisements, those on car 32 here being an exception. It is seen as fitted with a Mountain & Gibson Radial truck. In 1906, five cars were so converted but did not find lasting favour. In 1910, they were transferred to Coventry tramways where 32 become number 40. (East Anglia Transport Museum Collection)

104. Coventry car 38 was formerly Norwich no. 9. A number of modifications had been made by the time this picture was taken in May 1937. These included full canopies, new platforms and a conventional longer wheelbase Peckham P22 truck. The five ex-Norwich cars were still on the Coventry fleet strength when the 1940 Blitz brought tramway operation to a premature close.
(H.B. Priestley/National Tramway Museum)

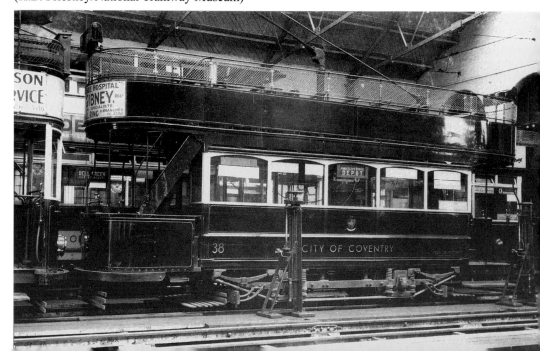

105. By 1929-30, nine of the original Brush cars had been refurbished, rather than replaced. The rebuilding included removal of the glass slide route indicator boxes and the substitution of a plain panel above each canopy. Illumination was also provided for the coloured route boards. These had been removed when this striking pose of car 31 was caught by the camera at Silver Road in 1935.
(Dr. H.A. Whitcombe/ Science Museum, Science & Society Picture Library)

106. The body of Brush car 39 still exists in a garden to the north of Norwich and has been off the rails since 1924. Its condition is a tribute to its builders and to those who have subsequently cared for it.
(Author)

107. An inside view of surviving car 39 shows the clerestory roof. More properly described as a monitor roof, it is indicative of American practice which still strongly influenced British tramcar construction in the late Victorian period. (Author)

108. One of the 1900 trailer cars (believed to be car 48) was pictured as a permanent way van at Silver Road Depot in 1932. (Dr Hugh Nicol/National Tramway Museum)

109. Five of the trailers were converted into powered cars in 1906; incorporating spare trucks, new controllers, lengthened platforms and larger fenders. Driver Barker and conductor Beaumont are seen here with car 47 in 1907. (Mrs A. Fothergill)

110. Four heavily touched pictures illustrate a snow plough which was constructed after the heavy snow fall of 1906. Car 47 was regularly on stand-by duties as a plough pusher, but was never called upon to cope with anything approaching the conditions of 1906.
(Tramway & Railway World)

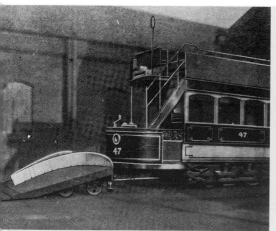

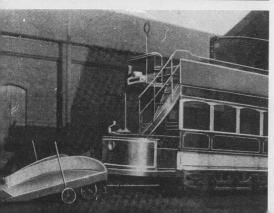

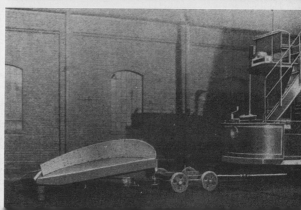

111. An overhauled Peckham cantilever truck is out on the depot approach. The point in the foreground has two blades and has been fabricated from Vignoles rail, rather than the usual British Standard grooved tramrail. Most street tramway installations had only one blade. (East Anglia Transport Museum collection)

112. Second generation car 39 is being off-loaded from a rail wagon at Norwich City Station in 1924. This was one of a batch of six which was, in turn, the third consignment from English Electric of Preston. (George Swain collection/NLIS)

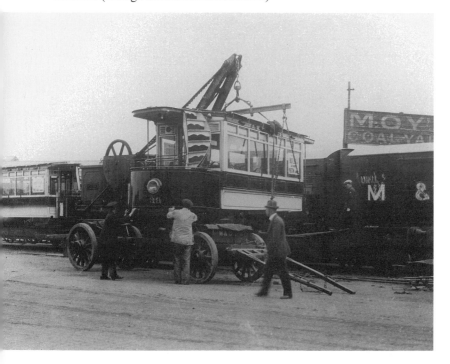

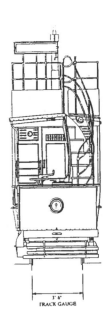

3' 6"
TRACK GAUGE

113.   English Electric car 15 is seen as delivered in 1928 and fitted to its rehabilitated 1900 Peckham truck. Smart but outdated, the whole assembly was an Edwardian echo. Further deliveries of this type were taken up to and including 1930. (English Electric/East Anglia Transport Museum)

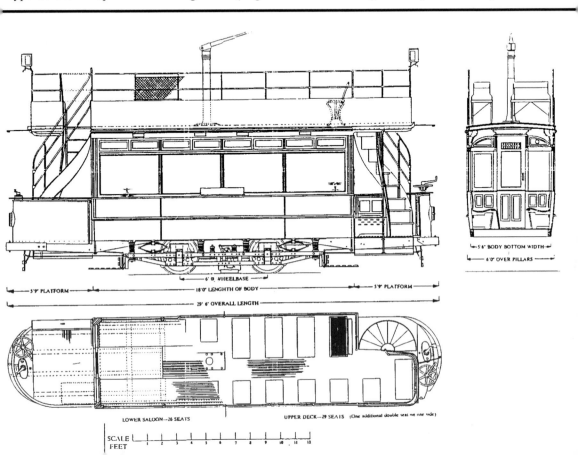

114.   The same car was recorded at the same spot but towards the end of its career, in 1935. It has been re-equipped to take coloured route boards and the roller blinds have been resited in the windows. Upper deck lanterns from a withdrawn Brush car have been added. (Dr. H.A. Whitcombe/Science Museum/Science & Society Picture Library)

115.   The interiors of the English Electric cars, trimmed in oak, were brighter and airier than those of the Brush cars. The notices on the doors invite passengers to make use of the tramway parcels service. (English Electric/East Anglia Transport Museum)

116. A detail of the platform of car 41. The English Electric cars had wooden electrical resistance boxes and tool lockers on both platforms. These cars also had advertisements painted on their lower (rocker) side panels in their first years of service. (East Anglia Transport Museum collection)

117. The platform of English Electric car 33 is seen from the top deck. The Dick Kerr type controllor is at the driver's left hand. To the right is the combined hand brake staff and track brake wheel. The driver's use of the chin strap is more likely to be a response to a windy day than to the speed of the tram! (Frank Neal/ George Swain collection/ NLIS)

FARES PLEASE

118. During World War I, lady clippies filled gaps in the ranks left by conductors serving in the armed forces. This lady holds the punch which registered the number of tickets issued. (Geoffrey Goreham collection)

119. This view of a Norwich tramways ticket cannister showing how reels of numbered tickets were inserted from one end and separated by cardboard discs. Similar cannisters were used in Coventry. (Author/East Anglia Transport Museum)

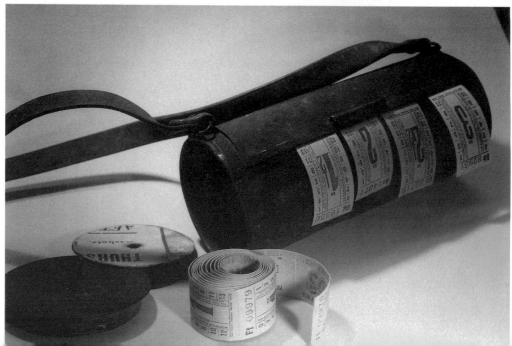

FINALE

120.   Final handover. Driver George Hill, oldest serving tram driver, symbolically grasps the hand of a busman on the night of 10th December 1935. To his right is Bernard Fisher, youngest conductor, who did a brisk trade in last tickets. Thirty five years of a safe and reliable service to the citizens of Norwich had come to an end. Some years later, George Hill's funeral cortege was to retrace the route of the Norwich trams' last run from Newmarket Road to the Silver Road depot via Orford Place. (Frank Neal/George Swain collection/NLIS)

Middleton Press

Easebourne Lane, Midhurst, W Sussex. GU29 9AZ Tel: 01730 813169 Fax: 01730 812601
If books are not available from your local transport stockist, order direct with cheque,
Visa or Mastercard, post free UK.

BRANCH LINES
Branch Line to Allhallows
Branch Line to Alton
Branch Lines around Ascot
Branch Line to Ashburton
Branch Lines around Bodmin
Branch Line to Bude
Branch Lines around Canterbury
Branch Lines around Chard & Yeovil
Branch Lines around Cromer
Branch Lines to East Grinstead
Branch Lines of East London
Branch Lines to Effingham Junction
Branch Lines around Exmouth
Branch Line to Fairford
Branch Lines around Gosport
Branch Line to Hawkhurst
Branch Lines to Horsham
Branch Lines around Huntingdon
Branch Line to Ilfracombe
Branch Line to Kingswear
Branch Lines to Launceston & Princetown
Branch Line to Longmoor
Branch Line to Looe
Branch Line to Lyme Regis
Branch Lines around March
Branch Lines around Midhurst
Branch Line to Minehead
Branch Line to Moretonhampstead
Branch Line to Padstow
Branch Lines around Plymouth
Branch Lines to Seaton and Sidmouth
Branch Line to Selsey
Branch Lines around Sheerness
Branch Line to Shrewsbury
Branch Line to Swanage *updated*
Branch Line to Tenterden
Branch Lines around Tiverton
Branch Lines to Torrington
Branch Lines to Tunbridge Wells
Branch Line to Upwell
Branch Lines of West London
Branch Lines around Weymouth
Branch Lines around Wisbech

NARROW GAUGE
Branch Line to Lynton
Branch Lines around Portmadoc 1923-46
Branch Lines around Porthmadog 1954-94
Branch Line to Southwold
Douglas to Port Erin
Kent Narrow Gauge
Two-Foot Gauge Survivors
Romneyrail
Southern France Narrow Gauge
Vivarais Narrow Gauge

SOUTH COAST RAILWAYS
Ashford to Dover
Bournemouth to Weymouth
Brighton to Eastbourne
Brighton to Worthing
Dover to Ramsgate
Eastbourne to Hastings
Hastings to Ashford
Portsmouth to Southampton
Southampton to Bournemouth

SOUTHERN MAIN LINES
Basingstoke to Salisbury
Bromley South to Rochester
Crawley to Littlehampton
Dartford to Sittingbourne
East Croydon to Three Bridges
Epsom to Horsham
Exeter to Barnstaple
Exeter to Tavistock
Faversham to Dover

London Bridge to East Croydon
Orpington to Tonbridge
Tonbridge to Hastings
Salisbury to Yeovil
Swanley to Ashford
Tavistock to Plymouth
Victoria to East Croydon
Waterloo to Windsor
Waterloo to Woking
Woking to Portsmouth
Woking to Southampton
Yeovil to Exeter

EASTERN MAIN LINES
Fenchurch Street to Barking
Ipswich to Saxmundham
Liverpool Street to Ilford

WESTERN MAIN LINES
Ealing to Slough
Ely to Kings Lynn
Exeter to Newton Abbot
Newton Abbot to Plymouth
Paddington to Ealing
Slough to Newbury

COUNTRY RAILWAY ROUTES
Andover to Southampton
Bath Green Park to Bristol
Bath to Evercreech Junction
Bournemouth to Evercreech Jn.
Cheltenham to Andover
Croydon to East Grinstead
Didcot to Winchester
East Kent Light Railway
Fareham to Salisbury
Frome to Bristol
Guildford to Redhill
Reading to Basingstoke
Reading to Guildford
Redhill to Ashford
Salisbury to Westbury
Stratford upon Avon to Cheltenham
Strood to Paddock Wood
Taunton to Barnstaple
Wenford Bridge to Fowey
Westbury to Bath
Woking to Alton
Yeovil to Dorchester

GREAT RAILWAY ERAS
Ashford from Steam to Eurostar
Clapham Junction 50 years of change
Festiniog in the Fifties
Festiniog in the Sixties
Isle of Wight Lines 50 years of change
Railways to Victory 1944-46
SECR Centenary album
Talyllyn 50 years of change
Yeovil 50 years of change

LONDON SUBURBAN RAILWAYS
Caterham and Tattenham Corner
Charing Cross to Dartford
Clapham Jn. to Beckenham Jn.
Crystal Palace (HL) & Catford Loop
East London Line
Finsbury Park to Alexandra Palace
Kingston and Hounslow Loops
Lewisham to Dartford
Lines around Wimbledon
London Bridge to Addiscombe
Mitcham Junction Lines
North London Line
South London Line
West Croydon to Epsom
West London Line
Willesden Junction to Richmond

London Suburban Railway continued .....
Wimbledon to Beckenham
Wimbledon to Epsom

STEAMING THROUGH
Steaming through Cornwall
Steaming through the Isle of Wight
Steaming through Kent
Steaming through West Hants
Steaming through West Sussex

TRAMWAY CLASSICS
Aldgate & Stepney Tramways
Barnet & Finchley Tramways
Bath Tramways
Bournemouth & Poole Tramways
Brighton's Tramways
Burton & Ashby Tramways
Camberwell & W.Norwood Tramway
Clapham & Streatham Tramways
Croydon's Tramways
Dover's Tramways
East Ham & West Ham Tramways
Edgware and Willesden Tramways
Eltham & Woolwich Tramways
Embankment & Waterloo Tramways
Enfield & Wood Green Tramways
Exeter & Taunton Tramways
Greenwich & Dartford Tramways
Hammersmith & Hounslow Tramway
Hampstead & Highgate Tramways
Hastings Tramways
Holborn & Finsbury Tramways
Ilford & Barking Tramways
Kingston & Wimbledon Tramways
Lewisham & Catford Tramways
Liverpool Tramways 1. Eastern Routes
Liverpool Tramways 2. Southern Routes
Liverpool Tramways 3. Northern Routes
Maidstone & Chatham Tramways
Margate to Ramsgate
North Kent Tramways
Norwich Tramways
Portsmouth's Tramways
Reading Tramways
Seaton & Eastbourne Tramways
Shepherds Bush & Uxbridge Tramwa
Southampton Tramways
Southend-on-sea Tramways
Southwark & Deptford Tramways
Stamford Hill Tramways
Twickenham & Kingston Tramways
Victoria & Lambeth Tramways
Waltham Cross & Edmonton Tramwa
Walthamstow & Leyton Tramways
Wandsworth & Battersea Tramways

TROLLEYBUS CLASSICS
Croydon Trolleybuses
Bournemouth Trolleybuses
Hastings Trolleybuses
Maidstone Trolleybuses
Reading Trolleybuses
Woolwich & Dartford Trolleybuses

WATERWAY ALBUMS
Kent and East Sussex Waterways
London to Portsmouth Waterway
West Sussex Waterways

MILITARY BOOKS
Battle over Portsmouth
Battle over Sussex 1940
Bombers over Sussex 1943-45
Bognor at War
Military Defence of West Sussex
Military Signals from the South Coas
Secret Sussex Resistance
Surrey Home Guard
Sussex Home Guard

OTHER RAILWAY BOOKS
Garraway Father & Son
Index to all Middleton Press stations
Industrial Railways of the South-East
South Eastern & Chatham Railways
London Chatham & Dover Railway
War on the Line (SR 1939-45)